Papa Bear and the Chicago Bears' Winning Ways

Patrick McCaskey

Sporting Chance Press

ISBN: 978-1-7345863-1-2

Sporting Chance Press™, Inc.
1074 Butler Drive
Crystal Lake, IL 60014
sportingchancepress.com

Photographs and illustrations appearing in *Papa Bear and the Chicago Bears Winning Ways* were sourced from the Library of Congress, the National Park Service, Bill Potter, and Daniel Norris. Please see the Photographs and Illustrations Credit Table on page 96 for more information.

The opinions and ideas expressed are those of the author who is entirely responsible for its content. The author has composed *Papa Bear and the Chicago Bears' Winning Ways* at his own expense, using his own resources and technology. This publication is not associated in any way with the Chicago Bears Football Team.

Introduction

Thank you for reading *Papa Bear and the Chicago Bears' Winning Ways*. As a Vice President of the Chicago Bears, Bears' history is important to me. I hope it is interesting to you.

My grandfather, George "Papa Bear" Halas, was the owner of the Chicago Bears and one of the founders of the National Football League (NFL). Halas was a wonderful grandfather and a great man. He accomplished so much in his lifetime that many books have been written about him. ***Papa Bear and the Chicago Bears' Winning Ways* is a book written for you.** It is about how Halas successfully managed the Bears during the 20th century. It's also a book that focuses on some of George Halas's sayings or "winning ways" that may inspire you in your own life.

People will sometimes face tough times. Habits that support good values or virtues can help you succeed through tough challenges.

Papa Bear and the Chicago Bears Winning Ways discusses historical events that affected George Halas and many others. The names of some of these events and people are put in *italics* and then we explain them for you in the Glossary in the back of the book. I hope you will like our *Winning Ways*. Go Bears!

CONTENTS

Author, Patrick McCaskey

Sometimes It's Okay to Be Late

In 1915, my grandfather, George Halas, worked for the *Western Electric* company during the summer while he was in college.

On Saturday, July 24, Western Electric employees were preparing to attend a company picnic in Michigan City, Indiana. Boats were scheduled to take employees from the Chicago lakefront to the all-day event. One boat was called the Eastland, which my grandfather was scheduled to take that morning. My grandfather *missed the boat*—he was late arriving at the lakefront after an older brother had him step on the scale at home to check his progress on his muscle-building program.

Before grandpa reached the lakefront, the Eastland tragically rolled over on its side and 844 people died. If he hadn't missed the boat, the National Football League, the Chicago Bears, and Patrick McCaskey might not be here.

My grandfather lettered in football, basketball, and baseball at the University of Illinois. He graduated with a degree in engineering in 1918. As a University of Illinois graduate, the school colors of navy blue and burnt orange would always be his favorite. Guess what the Bears colors are today?

Patrick McCaskey

World War I

When my grandfather was about to graduate from college, the United States entered World War I. World War I was especially brutal. It lasted in Europe from 1914-1918. It involved many countries and saw an especially horrific type of fighting called *trench warfare*. In trench warfare, both sides dug trenches to protect themselves at the *battlefront* from *artillery* and machine guns. When soldiers left the trenches to charge the enemy, many were killed and wounded. About 8-10 million men died and another 20 million were wounded during World War I.

Halas joined the Unites States Navy in 1918. The Navy was helping the allies bring needed supplies and men overseas. He entered officer candidate school. My grandfather was assigned to the Great Lakes Naval Station. He found that his athletic talents were in demand for conditioning men for combat, creating teamwork, and instilling pride and confidence through competition. He played on the Great Lakes Bluejackets military football team. They were an excellent team and they played in the *Rose Bowl*. Halas was voted most valuable player in the 1919 Rose Bowl!

Right after the War, Halas was asked to play right field for the 1919 New York Yankees. During his stay with the Yankees, he batted .091. He was having a hard time *"hitting the curveball."* He liked baseball, but he was excited about the growth of football. He played for the 1919 Hammond Pros football team that fall.

WINNING WAYS

WW I Poster by James Montgomery

Staleys

On March 18, 1920, George Chamberlain met with my grandfather in Chicago. Chamberlain was the general superintendent of the A. E. Staley Manufacturing Company in Decatur, Illinois. It was an *agribusiness* company that manufactured *starch* products. It would later develop a huge business with soy beans and sweeteners. Augustus Eugene Staley was the founder of the company. He wanted his employees to enjoy sports.

Chamberlain offered Halas the opportunity to learn the starch business and to be the company's football coach. He could also play on the Staley football and baseball teams. Later, he became the company's athletic director. At that time, football players needed full time jobs outside of sports to support themselves. Halas accepted the offer. Halas was given a job in the plant and time to practice on the athletic fields. In those days, many companies had their own sports teams. The sports headline in the March 19 *Decatur Daily Review* stated: "George 'Chic' Halas Joins Staley Forces."

Hupmobile

Hupmobile Showroom

Halas immediately began to recruit some of the best football players in the country for his Staley team. He had met many of them in college and in the Navy. Besides the challenge of recruiting good players, he had another big problem and that was scheduling games.

Having a football organization or *league* that was made up of teams was the way to solve scheduling problems. *NFL schedules* have evolved throughout its history.

On September 17, 1920, George Halas and a group of men met at Ralph Hay's *Jordan Hupmobile* car showroom in Canton, Ohio. The Library of Congress photo on the previous page shows the Hupmobile about the time George Halas was creating his team.

If you have not heard of the Hupmobile and the Jordan automobiles, chances are you have not heard of the Abbott, Auburn, Cole, Crow, Davis, Dixie, Durant, Elcar, Grant, King, Kline, Lafayette, Kurtz, Marmon, Mercer, Overland, Peerless, Pilot, Roamer, Saxon, Stearns, Velie, Wescott and Winton—all early car makers that merged or went out of business. You might catch a glimpse of these cars at a *vintage* auto show.

WINNING WAYS

Hay owned the Canton Bulldogs football team and he knew several other team owners. While sitting on the bumpers and *running boards* of the Jordan and Hupmobile cars, they organized the league that we call the National Football League today. The creation of this league is considered by most historians the beginning of professional football. There were teams affiliated with a town; semi-pro teams with some paid players and some that played for no pay; and teams that were sponsored by companies that would pay for uniforms and expenses. But the Canton meeting turned out to provide a clear line to distinguish the beginning of the pros. The first pro football season was 1920.

A year later in 1921, Mr. Staley discovered that teams needed bigger stadiums and larger crowds to earn enough money to pay the best players. When the economy saw a downturn, Mr. Staley gave my grandfather $5,000 to move the team to Chicago and take over ownership. Halas promised Mr. Staley that he would keep the Staley name for one year. So, in 1921, the team was called the Chicago Staleys. They won the first of nine championships (as the Staleys and then the Bears) that year. They played in the stadium called Cubs' Park that we call *Wrigley Field* today. In the winter of 1922, the team's name was changed to the Chicago Bears.

Midway Plaisance

Monsters of the Midway

If anyone could be called the Father of the NFL, it would be George Halas. In this way, his nickname Papa Bear says it all. He loved the fans and was dedicated to his players, friends, family, and faith. Halas worked non-stop for decades to make pro football work. No one worked as hard or as long as George Halas.

In time, the Bears became the *Monsters of the Midway*. The Midway Plaisance in Chicago is parkland a mile long and 220 yards wide that connects Washington and Jackson Parks. The photo on the previous pages shows what the Midway Plaisance looked like for the *World's Columbian Exposition*—a World's Fair that was established in honor of the 400-year anniversary of Columbus's discovery of America. The *Farris Wheel* in the photograph was the first one created. It was built and designed by George Washington Gale Farris.

Most of the finer buildings created for the fair were housed in a beautiful "White City" built in Jackson Park. The director of works for the Fair was famed architect Daniel Burnham. The exhibits on the Midway were created for entertainment and featured many attractions, stores, and places to buy food and drink. The term "midway" would be used afterward to describe the entertainment area of a fair or carnival. Once the fair ended, most of the buildings were taken down.

Some buildings built for the Fair remain. The Palace of Fine Arts for the fair is now the Museum of Science and Industry. The Art Institute of Chicago was another building created at the time of the fair. Both buildings and the surrounding areas have undergone many changes over the years.

The first team called the Monsters of the Midway was the squad of the *University of Chicago,* which was located in the Midway area. When the University stopped playing football, the nickname was used to describe the Bears.

When Halas's team became the Monsters of the Midway, it was like announcing to the World that they were the top football team in Chicago. Next, Halas worked tirelessly to see that the National Football League and that his team, the Chicago Bears, made it through the Great Depression and then World War II.

Great Depression

On October 29, 1929, the American Stock Market collapsed. The day became known as Black Tuesday. The economy performed poorly for the next decade—a period that became known as the *Great Depression*. Jobs were lost, businesses collapsed—even banks shut down. Many people became poor.

Americans struggled to find work. Some had to move to find work. Many went hungry.

Young Worker in 1930s, *Walker Evans* Photo

Abandoned Farm

Dust Bowl

As businesses suffered from the Great Depression, the weather also created a major *catastrophe* at that time. In the *Great Plains,* drought and poor soil conservation led to a huge *dust bowl.*

Large amounts of top soil took to the air and blew off farms and landed hundreds of mile away. The photo taken above by Arthur Rothstein is from the Library of Congress and it shows the damage caused during the dust bowl.

WINNING WAYS

With unemployment as high as 25%, George Halas somehow sold tickets to football games and tried to keep his players paid. How was he able to do it? Many people thought that America needed sports and entertainment especially at tough times. Halas heard firsthand from fans that sports can take people's minds off their troubles, at least for a few hours!

But football had problems around the turn of the Century before George Halas became involved and the Great Depression set in. Many people thought football was a *perilous* game—serious injuries occurred all too often. President *Theodore "Teddy" Roosevelt* worked to see football rules improved to make it safer in 1905. Teddy Roosevelt's distant cousin, *Franklin Delano Roosevelt* (FDR), became President during the Great Depression on March 4, 1933. FDR was taught with all his classmates at Groton School, a famous college preparatory school, that football was morally and physically important to a young man's development.

By the time George Halas got involved with football, he was impressed with how excited people were about the games and how well men could play it long after they graduated from college.

Patrick McCaskey

Fireside Chats

FDR's Radio Broadcast

Our country suffered through tough times when FDR was in office. He often gave talks on the radio that were meant to assure Americans that things would get better. These talks were called "Fireside Chats." Some people said that when they listened to the President on the radio, it was like he had come into their home and sat there in the living room with them next to a fireplace.

While Halas and millions of Americans were trying to make a living, Franklin Delano Roosevelt (FDR) introduced many programs in what was called his *New Deal*. In order to help the country pull out of the Depression, he focused on what was called the 3-Rs: relief, recovery, and reform. These programs helped give the country some direction and hope. Many of the programs were introduced and restructured as Roosevelt and his advisers and staff were looking for the best solutions.

Federal Emergency Management Relief Camp

Patrick McCaskey

World War II

USS Indianapolis

Ten years after the beginning of the Great Depression, World War II began in Europe in 1939. The United States got into the War after the bombing of *Pearl Harbor* on December 7, 1941. The United States declared War on Japan on December 8, 1941. Germany and Italy joined the conflict against the United States on the side of Japan on December 11.

After the United States entered the war, American forces were mobilized. A great number of men were entering the military. Halas and other NFL owners would face another period of great challenges. President Franklin Roosevelt would continue to serve as President until his death on April 12, 1945, towards the end of the war. Vice President *Harry Truman* would take over as President at that time.

WINNING WAYS

George Halas wanted to serve his country and went back into the Navy at age 47. Halas used his considerable organization skills serving *Admiral Kincaid* who was supporting *General Douglas MacArthur* in the *Pacific*. Once again, the Navy made use of Halas's leadership skills as recreation and welfare officer. Later he was promoted to *Commander Halas*.

Halas was getting men ready for their duties. World War II naval assignments would have included work on a variety of vessels. Many of the men would serve on battleships. These were immense heavily armored ships with large guns. The USS Indianapolis pictured on the previous page was one of these.

During World War II, many NFL teams took extraordinary cost cutting measures to make it through the war. The Pittsburgh Steelers and Philadelphia Eagles combined in 1943 to become the "Steagles." Then, in 1944 the Pittsburgh Steelers combined with the Chicago Cardinals to become the "Card-Pitts." Some fans called them the "Carpets"—their record was 0-10 that year.

Halas and other NFL owners faced many challenges during the war. Poor attendance and lack of qualified players were two of the greatest. The owners debated whether to continue play during the war, but they recognized in the end that the country needed such games as a morale booster. As the war was coming to an end in 1945, teams would go back to their old organizations.

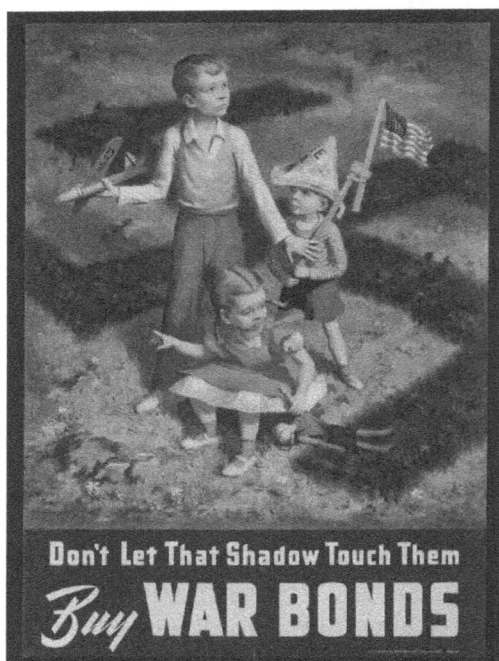

Don't Let That Shadow Touch Them
Buy WAR BONDS

WWII Poster by Lawrence Beall Smith

Once the War ended, professional football became more popular although there were certain *postwar difficulties for the NFL* that had be sorted out. Many innovations and plans put into place by George Halas helped make the game one of the most popular sports in America. Finally, when television generously supported the game, Halas could take a deep breath. He had worked very hard for about 30 years and the game was financially successful.

Statues at Soldier Field

Sometime we *commemorate* people and ideas in statues. Sports statues have meaning for fans and when they are placed on stadium campuses they add something powerful to the local culture. At the same time, they often mean something personal to those who see them.

The Chicago Bears unveiled statues of George Halas and Walter Payton on September 3, 2019, at the south entrance of Soldier Field. The unveiling coincided with the start of celebrations for the 100th NFL season.

My mother, Virginia McCaskey, spoke at the ceremony:

My brother and I used to ride in a car along the outer drive through the parks and see the statues in the park settings. It seemed like most of them were generals on horses, but we never dreamed that someday, our dad and a Chicago Bears player would be honored in the same way. We are very happy to be here.

Walter Payton's daughter, Brittney Payton, said:

We know that dad is definitely smiling down on all of us. And he would be so proud of this moment and moved beyond words.

The statues were created by sculptor Chad Fischer. The windy conditions along the Chicago Lakefront will not cause any problems for the structures, they are both 12 feet high and weigh 3,000 pounds.

Walking to Commemorate Papa Bear

In celebration of the 100th anniversary of the Bears, Chicago Bears Chairman George McCaskey walked from the original site of the Decatur Staleys football team to the team's home turf at Soldier Field. The 196-mile trek was made from July 15–25, 2019. The journey put him in touch *symbolically* with his grandfather George Halas—his struggle to manage the Chicago Bears from its early days in Decatur throughout its history in Chicago. Although symbolic, the trip involved a strenuous effort to complete.

Halas's "journey" with the Bears tested his faith and his faith gave him the strength to continue. The anniversary journey was a fitting "pilgrimage."

According to Bears Senior Writer, Larry Mayer, McCaskey started in Decatur; traveled to Champaign, home of Halas's University of Illinois college team; and then he moved on to the Bears Bourbonnais training camp at Olivet Nazarene University. From Bourbonnais, it was on to Midway Airport then through the city to Soldier Field. McCaskey walked by himself. Training since the beginning of the year, McCaskey managed roughly 20 miles a day.

Halas's Players

George Halas drove hundreds of athletes to make them the best players and men they could be. And for the first decade of the NFL, he played, coached, and owned the team. As a player, Halas broke his jaw and his leg, he twisted ankles and knees, and bruised and broke ribs. He led his teams as a players' coach and although he was tough and disciplined, he always treated his players as men.

Prior to the start of the 1968 season, Halas retired from coaching after 40 seasons. Some of the Bears great players are discussed in this section. Most are players that Halas knew and recruited, but we have included some more recent Bears. All those listed are the kind of players that Papa Bear would have approved.

George Trafton

Hall of Famer George Trafton was a 6–foot–2, 230 pound bull who loved to mix it up. Trafton played center for the Staleys/Bears right from the start in 1920. He took a year off to coach at Northwestern and then played from 1922-1932.

Sports writers sometimes deliberately exaggerate to entertain their readers—this is called *hyperbole*. Trafton was once described by a reporter as someone who was disliked in every NFL city with the exception of Green Bay and Rock Island—in those cities he was hated. Trafton was inducted into the Hall of Fame in 1964.

Red Grange, the Galloping Ghost

Red Grange

Red Grange was a great college player at the University of Illinois. He worked hard as a boy in Wheaton, Illinois. During the summers he delivered feed, coal, and huge blocks of ice. Grange would be called "The Ice Man." At Wheaton High School, he played football, basketball, track, and baseball. Later he was called "The Galloping Ghost" because no one seemed to be able to tackle him—it was as if he was a spirit.

Grange was the most famous football player of his time. Certainly by today's standards he would be called a superstar. Pro football was not very popular before Halas was able to get Grange to play for the Bears. Grange began his pro career on Thanksgiving Day, November 26, 1925. At this time, the newspapers were still the major source of news. Radio was in its early years. Television was a long way off and the Internet over half a century into the future.

After Grange joined the Bears, the team went on a special tour to different cities all over the country so people could see the great star in person. Just a few years earlier, Halas had to work hard just to get the newspapers to cover the Bears. Now, many of the top sports reporters followed the Bears tour. Many people believe that Grange helped the NFL stay in business because he sold so many tickets everywhere he played. Grange was enshrined in Pro Football Hall of Fame's charter (first) class of 1963.

Bronislaw "Bronko" Nagurski

Halas attracted the toughest of players. *Bronko Nagurski* was one such player. For many years, football players played on both defense and offense. Nagurski ran over players as a fullback and he mowed down players as a linebacker.

Nagurski played during the Depression when times were tough for everyone even star football players. The team with the best record was awarded the NFL championship in the early days, but the Bears were tied with the Portsmouth Spartans at season end in 1932, so a championship game was held.

The game was held in Chicago, but horrific weather sent the teams indoors to the Chicago Stadium. The game was played on a short field. The Bears triumphed, 9–0. The game featured a play in which Nagurski faked a run and then stepped back and threw a jump-pass to Grange for a touchdown.

Nagurski was one of the most popular players of the 1930s. General Mills put his illustrated biography on a Wheaties box. Nagurski was enshrined in Pro Football Hall of Fame's charter class of 1963.

Sid Luckman

Although the T Formation had been one of the oldest formations in football, Halas and his coaches had been experimenting with modifications in the 1930s. Halas's friend Clark Shaughnessy worked with his staff to design and implement a version of the T Formation that would make use of man in motion and other elements. It was a *Modified T Formation* that was much more difficult to defend.

To run this complex offense, Halas recruited an especially smart quarterback from Columbia University, Sid Luckman, who joined the team in 1939. Halas also had a number of tremendous players heading into the 1940 season including Hall of Famers Clyde "Bulldog" Turner and George McAfee.

The NFL was broken down into two divisions. At season end, the first-place Bears of the West Division played the first place Washington Redskins of the East Division in the NFL Championship game. The Bears won the game, 73–0, in the largest scoring game of all time. About that time, the song "Bear Down Chicago Bears" was written, which included the line: "We'll never forget the way you thrilled the nation with your 'T' formation." Luckman was enshrined in Pro Football Hall of Fame's class of 1965.

George Connor

The Bears signed legendary Notre Dame Lineman George Connor in 1948. Connor originally went to Holy Cross, served in the military during the war, and then played for the University of Notre Dame. The Fighting Irish won two consecutive national championships with Connor and another future Bear, Johnny Lujack.

The Bears had to stop a powerful Philadelphia Eagles running attack in 1949 and they turned to Connor, who was an agile, fast 6–foot–3, 240 pound tackle. He was moved to linebacker by Halas and staff. His success there helped establish a larger *prototype* for that position—Connor had the essential features of players who would have that position in the future. The Bears became known for their great linebackers: Bill George, Dick Butkus, Doug Buffone, Mike Singletary, Brian Urlacher, and others.

Connor was enshrined in Pro Football Hall of Fame's class of 1975.

Doug Atkins

Hall of Famer Doug Atkins was a giant defensive end for his era at 6–foot–8 and 257 pounds—a true Monster of the Midway. He played for the Bears from 1955-1966. Atkins posed the greatest challenge to offensive lines and quarterbacks. Having a track and basketball background, he could leap over blockers, extend his arms to control large swaths of running lanes, and block passes from heights unseen.

The toughest of men on the field, Atkins was also tough to coach, but Halas managed the big man very well from 1955-1966. Atkins was enshrined in Pro Football Hall of Fame's of 1982.

Mike Ditka

Tight end Mike Ditka was a gifted athlete and spirited competitor who was Rookie-of-the-Year in 1961. Ditka had size, power, skill, and desire. The 6–foot–3, 228 pound Ditka impressed football opponents with excellent receiving skills, the strength of an interior lineman, and the running ability of a halfback.

Ditka played for the Bears from 1961-1966 including the 1963 Championship Season. He returned as head coach in 1982 to lead the Bears to their Super Bowl XX Championship with the 1985 Bears. He was enshrined in Pro Football Hall of Fame's class of 1988.

Dick Butkus

Raised in the Chicago neighborhood of Roseland, Dick Butkus was a big fan of football at an early age. Like Halas, Butkus attended the University of Illinois.

Hall of Famer Dick Butkus was one of the most intimidating players in the NFL when he played middle linebacker for the Bears from 1965-1973. At the snap of the ball, he attacked the opposing team and clawed at anyone in his way in a frenzied pursuit of running backs and quarterbacks. Butkus was the perfect successor of all the toughest Bears who had gone before him including Halas himself. He was enshrined in Pro Football Hall of Fame's class of 1979.

Gale Sayers

Called the Kansas Comet, Gale Sayers was a running back for the Chicago Bears from 1965-1971. Sayers entertained football fans with his acrobatic and powerful running style. His performance wowed football fans that were starting to follow the game on television in increasing numbers.

Every time Sayers handled the ball, his performance could end up on the highlight reel. Sayers was an All-Pro for 5 seasons. His brilliant career lasted 5 full seasons and 2 brief ones. He was inducted into the Pro Football Hall of Fame in 1977.

Mike Singletary

Mike Singletary, Hall of Famer middle linebacker played for the Bears from 1981-1992. Famous for his mastery of game, courageous play, and intensity—Singletary was the defensive leader of the Bears in the 1980s including the team's NFL Championship season in 1985. Singletary was the NFL Defensive Player of the Year for 1985. He was inducted into the Hall of Fame in 1998.

From his position in the center of the action on the field, viewers saw Singletary look out like a hawk, size up the possible movements of the offense, and bark out instructions to his teammates. His routine was so much fun to watch, the Bears defense received plenty of camera time in games and on highlight films.

Walter "Sweetness" Payton

Hall of Famer Walter Payton has been described by many as simply the best football player of all time. That is not an exaggeration. He could run, block, catch, pass, punt, and kick. There was nothing in football he could not do.

Fans loved to watch Sweetness run through a hole in the defensive line and then run over defensive backs and even linebackers like a tank.

Payton was a magnificent athlete. He missed one game in his entire pro career and trained with legendary discipline and intensity—coming into each training camp in superb condition. Payton was also a beloved Bear and respected by those throughout the league. Football fans from all over the country were his fans. The outstanding running back played for the Bears from 1975-1987. He was enshrined in Pro Football Hall of Fame's class of 1993.

Brian Urlacher

Brian Urlacher was a small boy when George Halas died, but he was exactly the kind of player that Halas would have signed. He played for the Bears from 2000-2012. He was the first remarkable Bears Middle Linebacker of the 21st century. A big strong athlete who was freakishly fast and agile for his size. Urlacher could clog up the middle and stop the run as well as guard receivers like a defensive back.

Urlacher played all his 13 seasons with the Chicago Bears. Right from the start, he was a star—he won the Rookie-of-the-Year award in 2000. He was the NFL Defensive Player of the Year in 2005 and he was selected to eight Pro Bowls. Urlacher was enshrined in Pro Football Hall of Fame's class of 2018.

Urlacher was one of the most popular modern players due in part to his competitive smart play that he matched with a clean approach to the game.

Halas in History

George Halas is a larger-than-life figure for many sports fans. Although his life was hard, it was fantastic on so many levels. His life's story is a living history of *20th Century America*. Stamped upon his character were lessons from the *Great Depression, World War I,* and *World War II.*

In so many ways, his life was successful because he had faith, worked hard, and never gave up. He saw problems as opportunities. He moved on from setbacks at lightning speed. In Chicago, sportswriter Warren Brown wrote a book named after his long running *Chicago American* newspaper column, *Win, Lose, or Draw.* In books like this, the sports writer would often name his favorite people in sport. Brown described his favorite this way:

> In the professional field George Halas
> and the Chicago Bears year in and year
> out, will do for me. I am not too hard to
> please as long as I have the best, doing
> anything.

Brown received the J. G. Taylor Spink Award, the highest award given by the Baseball Writers' Association of America.

Halas Highlights

George Halas coached for 40 seasons. He holds an overall NFL head coaching record of 324–151–31. The Bears won six NFL Championships with Halas as coach and a total of eight as NFL owner. Halas was present at the beginning of the NFL and worked tirelessly for over 60 years to see professional football succeed. Halas was named AP Coach of the Year, the Sporting News Coach of the Year, and the UPI NFL Coach of the Year for both 1963 and 1965. He was enshrined in Pro Football Hall of Fame's charter class of 1963.

Halas Timeline

1895
February 2, 1895, George Stanley Halas is born in Chicago.

1913
Halas graduates from Crane Tech High School in Chicago where he set many track records, and played baseball and lightweight football.

1914-1918
Halas attends the University of Illinois and plays football, basketball, and baseball.

1918
Halas joins the Navy and serves at Great Lakes Naval Station as recreation officer. He serves as player-coach of Great Lakes Bluejackets football team.

1919
January 1, 1919, Halas is named Most Valuable Player in the Rose Bowl. He scores on a 45-yard touchdown pass from Paddy Driscoll and he runs back an interception 77 yards in the Great Lakes' 17–0 victory over the Mare Island Marines.

Halas plays for the New York Yankees and their Minor League *affiliate*.

Halas plays for the Hammond Pros semipro football team.

1920
Halas is hired by A.E. Staley to manage and coach the Decatur Staleys football team.

September 17, 1920, Halas attends the original pro football organizational meeting in Canton at the Jordan Hupmobile showroom of Ralph E. Hay, owner of the Canton Bulldogs. Halas, Hay, and others who were present establish the American Professional Football Association.

1921
October 6, 1921, a letter agreement from A.E. Staley formally turns ownership of the Staley team to George Halas. Halas becomes owner of the Staleys.

Chicago Staleys capture the APFA (NFL) championship with a 9–1–1 record—it is Halas's first championship as a coach and owner.

1922
Halas's team becomes the Chicago Bears.

Halas's proposal to change the league name from the American Professional Football Association to the National Football League is accepted by membership.

1930
Halas steps down as Bears' coach and Ralph Jones replaces him for the 1930-1932 seasons.

1932
Chicago Bears, coached by Jones, capture the NFL championship with a 7–1–6 record.

1933
The NFL creates the East and West Divisions, and establishes a post season game between the top finishers in each to determine the league champion.

December 17, 1933, the Halas-coached Chicago Bears defeat the New York Giants, 23–21, to win the NFL championship.

1934
December 9, 1934, the New York Giants defeat the Chicago Bears, 30–13, in the NFL Championship game

that came to be called the "Sneakers Game." The Giants' come-from behind victory is in part facilitated by their use of basketball sneakers for better traction.

1940

December 8, 1940, the Chicago Bears defeat the Washington Redskins, 73–0, to win the NFL Championship. The Bears' modified T Formation proves to be unstoppable that day.

1941

December 21, 1941, the Chicago Bears defeat the New York Giants, 37–9, to win the NFL Championship.

1942

Halas returns to the Navy to serve for the duration of World War II. The Bears are coached by Hunk Anderson and Luke Johnsos during this period.

December 13, 1942, the Washington Redskins defeat the Chicago Bears, 14–6, to win the NFL championship.

1943

December 26, 1943, the Chicago Bears defeat the Washington Redskins, 41–21, to win the NFL Championship. It is the Bears' third championship in four seasons.

1946

Halas returns to coach the Bears. December 15, 1946, the Bears defeat the New York Giants, 24–14, to win the NFL championship.

1956

Halas steps down from coaching for the 1956 and 1957 seasons. Paddy Driscoll takes over as head coach.

1963

Halas is enshrined into the Pro Football Hall of Fame as part of the charter class of 17 members.

December 29, 1963, the Bears defeat the New York Giants, 14–10, to win the NFL championship. It is Halas's sixth NFL Championship as coach and his eighth as owner.

Halas is named AP Coach of the Year, the Sporting News Coach of the Year, and the UPI NFL Coach of the Year for 1963.

1965

Halas is named AP Coach of the Year, the Sporting News Coach of the Year, and the UPI NFL Coach of the Year for 1965.

1968

Halas steps down from coaching for the last time. Jim Dooley takes over as Bears' head coach.

1983

October 31, 1983, George Halas dies at the age of 88.

Halas's Winning Ways

The Bears won the 1921, 1932, 1933, 1940, 1941, 1943, 1946, 1963, and 1985 championships. The Super Bowl began in 1967 (for the 1966 season championship). The 1985 season championship was also a Super Bowl win. As a coach, Halas won six championships. He won eight as an owner.

My grandfather, George Halas, was an optimist—he looked at things positively and found ways to bring out the best in himself and others. America needed optimists as it battled through the Great Depression and two world wars during the 20th century. Those who knew my grandfather would tell you that he lived life with a passion every day and seldom looked back. He was not a philosopher. His focus was always on football. But he did have a gift for providing support and encouragement. You will find Halas quotes in books and on the Internet. Here are some of my favorite along with my thoughts on them. These might help you.

"Don't do anything in practice that you wouldn't do in the game."

Hard work has its rewards. Halas came from a family that believed in hard work. He had no interest in wasting time because he believed there was no time for it. If you were wasting time, you were taking away time that you needed to apply elsewhere. And when he brought his team together, he wanted no wasted motions. When you waste time in practice, you waste it for everyone present.

When you decide not to waste time, you become **industrious**. You focus on accomplishment.

"Find out what the other team wants to do. Then take it away from them."

In competition of any kind, an opponent sets out to defeat you. And according to Halas, the best way to defeat competition is to stop them from doing what they want. If your opposition likes to run, you stop their running game. If they like to pass, you stop their passing game. If they win by taking advantage of your mistakes, you cut out the mistakes.

Some people do not like competition, but it is part of life. You have to be resolute or **determined** to compete and you must be courageous. In playing sports, you are practicing the good habits of these virtues.

"Many people flounder about in life because they do not have a purpose, an objective toward which to work."

A good coach likes to stick with a game plan, but the best coaches like to win. The best coaches have goals and they move forward from there. When Halas started out as the manager and coach of the Staleys, his objective was to build the best team. When the Staleys were turned over to Halas, his objective was to make the Staleys a success financially and on the field. When Halas found himself at the center of a new professional football league, his objective was to make the new league a success. He was building a team, developing a winning program, and establishing a viable league—all at once. Halas **set goals** and then he worked towards **achieving** them.

Halas was fierce after a loss—his wrath was legendary, but it lasted for a short time. Regardless of a game's outcome, Halas put it behind him and started thinking about next week's opponent. Halas like to ask after a tough loss, *"who do we play next week?"*

"If you live long enough, lots of nice things happen."

George Halas took very good care of himself. He watched his diet and he got good exercise. Good goals and hard work led to success, but he also believed it was important to live long to see the success! Like many former football players, Halas had his share of wounds, some of which would dog him for the rest of his life, but he set out to do his best to maintain his health in ways that he could. While much of the world was still thinking about retirement at age 65, Halas was coaching into his 70s and he managed the Bears well into his 80s.

Halas was resilient. He was determined to succeed. He had **fortitude**.

"Nobody who ever gave his best regretted it."

In sports, it is common knowledge that the best teams are highly principled and the best coaches are hard to please. Great effort makes the most sense after the performance, after the win. Regret comes with falling short, but satisfaction comes with *optimum* effort. Give your best, you won't regret it. Halas always approached life with his best **effort**.

"Nothing is work unless you'd rather be doing something else."

The most satisfying efforts are those that we take on without regret. The hungry athlete takes on exercise, study, training and repetition with satisfaction knowing that these things are leading to goals and objectives. If an athlete no longer shares his or her team's goals and *aspirations*, training becomes work. The athlete must overcome his opponents, but the most difficult thing to overcome is one's own *misgivings*. The athlete must be **motivated** and inspired.

Smart professional athletes also understand that at some point in an athlete's career, it is time to move on.

Confident President Barack Obama

"Never go to bed a loser."

We should never go to bed without having done what
we can to make our lives successful and feeling like a
success. We all lose at times, but a loser is someone
with a damaged ego, who believes himself to be a loser.
Halas would say that you should never accept those
kind of self-doubts. Do your best and believe that you
are a winner and you will be one. **Confidence** is
critical to all that we do.

BENJAMIN FRANKLIN
Peint d'après nature pour la Famille

Benjamin Franklin

Patrick McCaskey

Ben Franklin's Chart on Virtues

My grandfather was born over a hundred years ago. In a sense, his winning ways were a short list (not all) of the virtues that he practiced. A virtue is a trait or quality that people express or live by that is thought to be good or valued.

About the time our country was getting started, Ben Franklin, one of our country's founding fathers and "thought leaders," wrote about creating virtuous habits. This information was part of the "Autobiography of Ben Franklin," one of the greatest books ever written.

Franklin was not only a great thinker, he was accomplished in many pursuits. Franklin knew that he needed to work on forming good habits if he was going to improve and accomplish goals. As a means of self-help, Franklin created sheets that he used to record his work on virtues. Franklin created a list of virtues that he identified through his reading and research: temperance, silence, order, resolution, frugality, industry, sincerity, justice, moderation, cleanliness, tranquility, chastity, and humility.

Franklin wanted to focus on one virtue for at least a week. He wanted to create a habit practicing the virtue. He created a weekly chart with the name of one virtue and its definition at the top. Below the virtue, written or printed in a row, he created a square or cell for each day of the week. Then he included a column running down the left side of the chart with the first letter of all the virtues. The chart was filled out with blank boxes or cells. Each evening, he examined his conscience and he marked the boxes adjacent to the virtues where his performance was weak. He examined each virtue every day, but his focus was doing well on the "virtue of the week."

Halas's Winning Ways Chart

Applying Franklin's system to Halas's winning ways yields the charts below. Like Benjamin Franklin, you can use these charts to track your efforts to create habits of virtue.

Focus on one virtue each week and every night take some time to evaluate how you did. If you need to improve, place a check mark in the box under the day of the week in the row for that virtue. For days when you did well, put a star. For the first week, you are focusing on "Industrious," but go ahead mark how you did for the other virtues as well.

Week One

For the first week, each night you might ask yourself: Did I focus on accomplishment or did I spend too much time trying to entertain myself?

Industrious Focus on accomplishment to succeed							
	S	M	T	W	T	F	S
I							
D							
G							
F							
E							
M							
C							

I-Industrious, D-Determination, G-Goal Oriented, F-Fortitude, E-Effort, M-Motivated, C-Confident

Week Two

For the second week, each night you might want to ask yourself: What good things did I attempt to do but gave up on? Work on creating the habit of following through— of taking projects on with determination. Work on simple things at first and the habit will carry you through for tougher situations in the future. Become the person that others can count on to get things done.

Determination Be resolute and courageous to succeed						
	S	M	T	W	T	F	S
D							
G							
F							
E							
M							
C							
I							

D-Determination, G-Goal Oriented, F-Fortitude, E-Effort, M-Motivated, C-Confident, I-Industrious

Week Three

For the third week, each night you might want to ask yourself: What are those things in the back of my mind that I might want to accomplish, but I have never taken the time to write them out or work out a plan to get them done? Generally, it works to write your goals down and plan how you are going to accomplish them. Setting goals doesn't have to be painful, it just takes a little time. Once you form the habit of having success, you can move from small things to larger goals.

Goal Oriented Create goals and accomplish them to succeed							
	S	M	T	W	T	F	S
G							
F							
E							
M							
C							
I							
D							

G-Goal Oriented, F-Fortitude, E-Effort, M-Motivated, C-Confident, I-Industrious, D-Determination,

Week Four

For the fourth week, each night you might want to ask yourself: How am I doing on the things that take a longer time to accomplish? Fortitude is needed to achieve goals over a long period. In week 2, you looked at being determined to succeed. Some goals require a longer time—these require determination at the start but fortitude to finish. People make New Year resolutions that they start with great energy but give up on them. You don't train for a marathon or learn how to paint or speak a new language overnight, but you can create a plan to follow to get the job done! Work on developing fortitude to finish your long term tasks. Remember, once you create the habit, you will find you can accomplish bigger tasks down the road.

Fortitude Have endurance to succeed						
	S	M	T	W	T	F	S
F							
E							
M							
C							
I							
D							
G							

F-Fortitude, E-Effort, M-Motivated, C-Confident, I-Industrious, D-Determination, G-Goal Oriented

Week Five

For the fifth week, you might want to ask yourself: Did I put forth my best effort to succeed at my tasks, projects, sports, and school work. Or did I fall short and find myself thinking that's good enough for this activity?

George Halas knew that giving all work and activities his best effort was something to be achieved and a habit that needed to be formed. When we form the habit of giving our best, we just do it regularly and consistently. We can feel good about our accomplishments, but at the same time we shouldn't blame ourselves or feel bad when we have given our best and come up short. At times like that, we should pick ourselves up and look forward to the next game, contest, season, etc.

Many people do a good job with tasks they enjoy but deliver sloppy work on others. Make the effort to be more consistent and give all the good things you do, your best.

Effort Give your best effort to succeed						
	S	M	T	W	T	F	S
E							
M							
C							
I							
D							
G							
F							

E-Effort, M-Motivated, C-Confident, I-Industrious, D-Determination, G-Goal Oriented, F-Fortitude

Week Six

For the sixth week, you might want to ask yourself: How am I feeling about the tasks, activities, sports, and school projects that I am working on?

George Halas knew that motivated enthusiastic players were better players. When we learn to show enthusiasm for the good things we do, we find ourselves being a better classmate, teammate, and friend. We inspire others. We all need a little inspiration and that carries us through on the toughest of jobs. Once we form the habit of taking things on with enthusiasm, it will help us to be a more positive person.

Some people complain, criticize, and mope about many things. Stay motivated and be inspired to succeed. It isn't always easy, but you can create the good habit of seeing the positive.

Motivation Be inspired to succeed							
	S	M	T	W	T	F	S
M							
C							
I							
D							
G							
F							
E							

M-Motivated, C-Confident, I-Industrious, D-Determination, G-Goal Oriented, F-Fortitude, E-Effort

Week Seven

For the seventh week, you might want to ask yourself: How confident am I about those activities that I am working on? We often lack confidence doing things that we **can** achieve. Jump right in, try them, and work to improve. If it is something tough, then working to improve will require effort that will build confidence.

Once you put the time and effort into something, the nerves often disappear because your focus is on what it is you are doing not the audience. Certain coaches are so tough on players that when it comes time for the game, the players say that "anything is easier than practice," and the nerves melt away. Building a habit of confidence is about putting in the time to learn and sharpen the skills required for the task and just doing it.

Confidence Be self-assured to succeed						
	S	M	T	W	T	F	S
C							
I							
D							
G							
F							
E							
M							

C-Confident, I-Industrious, D-Determination, G-Goal Oriented, F-Fortitude, E-Effort, M-Motivated

More on Competition

People grow up with different skills and abilities. Their own interests will lead them to some activities more than others. Some adults find themselves enjoying sports more than when they were young. This is often because they have found something challenging yet fulfilling—they are motivated.

Football was Papa Bear's calling, but he did many other things outside of football in his life. He applied discipline to most everything he did. He negotiated contracts, wrote articles for the newspaper, and managed several businesses.

If you develop good habits of behavior you will likely have some success whether it is in sports, work, hobbies, and other activities.

In sports, maybe you will become a skilled shortstop or an awesome point guard. Or you might find that you enjoy running or long walks in which you compete most with yourself. People who are involved in many fitness activities today will keep track of their "personal best" record. For them, competition is often with themselves. Being involved in sports helps them improve their health and better health can improve almost everything they do.

Schools want you to be involved in something extra outside your studies. Good habits can help you. Put some effort into what you do and it will help you build confidence and achieve success.

Rest of this Story

My parents gave me plenty of good advice and inspiration. In the spring of my sophomore year at Notre Dame High School, I was perhaps a little too intense and my classmates did not seem to like me. I wanted to transfer. When I talked to my parents about it, they suggested that I talk with my grandfather, Papa Bear.

After my grandfather had heard me out, he looked me in the eye and said, "This is a small test. If you run from this, you'll run when something really difficult happens later in your life. Those fellows are jealous of you because you have a lot of talent. So get in there and show them."

I followed his advice and stayed at Notre Dame. If I had transferred, I would have missed being on the 1966 team that was 9-0 and outscored opponents 341-80.

Six of us started games on defense and offense. Greg Luzinski played linebacker and fullback. Pete Newell played defensive tackle and offensive tackle. Mike Newton played defensive back and offensive back. Ken Powers played linebacker and tight end. Mike Shaw played defensive tackle and center. I was the defensive signal caller and I played linebacker and quarterback.

I learned about leadership from our co-captains: Ken Powers and Mike Shaw. Ken led the team in tackles and he did impersonations of the characters in "The Wizard of Oz." Mike had poems published in the school literary magazine, "Vision." In track, I was a co-captain and I ran the two-mile and the mile.

After high school, I planned to go to Cheshire Academy in Connecticut in the fall to take some extra courses and get more football experience before college. During the summer, I was experiencing problems with my vision. After some tests, contact sports like football were prohibited. My eye doctor, George Jessen, asked me, "How much does your football career mean to you?"

I replied, "It means a lot to me."

He asked, "Does it mean so much to you that you'd risk losing your sight?"

I replied, "No."

Instead of playing football for Cheshire Academy, I ran cross-country. I won nine out of 13 races, including the conference championship. I was 14th in the New England Championships and won a medal.

In college, I spent much of my energy in reading and writing. I also pursued performance art and public speaking. All these skills I have used in my career with the Chicago Bears.

My grandfather's winning ways can help you create habits that support virtue and help lead you to success.

But if ever things get especially tough, make sure you talk to your parents and other people you can trust.

I hope you enjoyed the first half of *Papa Bear and the Chicago Bears Winning Ways*. My grandfather was important to Chicago, the Bears, the NFL, and me.

The next part of this book includes features that expand on ideas and events in the book: A glossary, quiz and discussion questions, and another exercise based on Ben Franklin's work.

Glossary

Admiral Kinkaid

Thomas Cassin Kinkaid served as an admiral in the United States Navy during World War II. A series of important commands led to him becoming the Commander Allied Naval Forces and the Seventh Fleet under General Douglas MacArthur in the South West Pacific Area. He commanded an Allied fleet during the Battle of Leyte Gulf, the largest naval battle of World War II.

A. E. Staley Manufacturing Company

A. E. Staley purchased a defunct starch-making plant in 1909 and opened its doors for business in 1912. Located in Decatur, Illinois, the A. E. Staley Manufacturing Company would eventually operate many plants across the country. In addition to starch products, Staley would developed sweeteners, soy bean products, and much more. Another agribusiness company, Tate & Lyle, purchased 90% of A. E. Staley in 1988 and the balance in 2000.

Affiliate

An affiliate is a person or organization officially attached to a larger body. Halas played for a minor league baseball team that was an affiliate of the New York Yankees.

Agribusiness

Agribusiness is the business of agricultural production which consists of many types of farming-related companies/organizations reaching out to include work that is done with farm produce to get it out to the marketplace. Farm equipment companies, seed companies, and companies that develop new food resources are examples of agribusinesses. Agribusinesses can employ chemists, engineers, economists, and other professionals as well as more traditional farming workers. Others involved in marketing, accounting, law and more work for agribusiness companies. Agribusiness is challenging and essential.

Artillery

Artillery is a classification of heavy weapons that are usually moved on wheels or tracks because they are too heavy to carry into battle. They can be used at a greater distance than the weapons used by individual soldiers. Artillery also includes large weapons on ships and large stationary weapons used to defend forts or other immobile military properties. Some members of the military specialize in artillery operations.

Aspirations

Aspirations are conditions or qualities that we want to achieve—something that we seek. Athletes have aspirations to achieve goals that support their team. Students have aspirations to prepare well for careers and life after school.

Battlefront

The forward area or place where opposing armies meet in combat is the battlefront.

Black Tuesday

Black Tuesday was the day the stock market crashed: October 29, 1929. It began the Great Depression.

Catastrophe

A catastrophe is a sudden disastrous event that causes great misfortune, suffering, or ruin. The Dust Bowl was one catastrophe that Americans endured during another catastrophe, the Great Depression.

Commander

Commander is an officer rank in the U. S. Navy. A Commander often serves as the captain of a small vessel, in charge of a small shore mission, or serves on the staff of a senior officer aboard a large vessel. George Halas held the rank of Commander.

Commemorate

Commemorate is to honor the memory of someone or something usually through some action or ceremony. Lincoln's Gettysburg Address was delivered at the dedication of the Soldiers National Cemetery to commemorate the Battle of Gettysburg.

Decatur Daily Review

The Decatur Daily Review began in October 1878. Another Decatur newspaper, *The Decatur Herald*, began in 1883. Both were in operation when the Decatur Staleys were playing in 1920. Newspapers were the main source of news at the time. Radio was in its early days and television was decades away. The two newspapers combined in 1931. *The Decatur Herald* became Decatur's morning paper and *The Decatur Daily Review* became Decatur's evening paper. In 1980, ownership of the newspapers combined them into one daily publication: *Herald & Review*.

Douglas MacArthur

Douglas MacArthur lived his entire life in the army and played important roles in World War I, World War II, and the Korean War. Every bit a scholar and gentleman, MacArthur was a graduate of the United States Military Academy at West Point. As a brigadier general in World War I, he led his men in France and became the most decorated soldier in the War.

He became superintendent of West Point following the war and then moved on to command the Army's Philippine Department. He became the Army Chief of Staff, the highest job in the service, and found himself back in the Philippines. At the start of World War II, when the Japanese invaded the Philippines,

MacArthur's forces were poorly matched and he was ordered to Australia. His famous words, "I shall return" was his bold promise to return, which he did three years later with a well-armed force. When the war in the Pacific ended, MacArthur was present at the surrender. After the war, as Supreme Commander to Allied Forces in Japan, he helped the Japanese recover and become financially sound.

When the Korean War began, MacArthur led an American-led coalition of United Nations forces and outmaneuvered the North Koreans in a bold amphibious assault. But when MacArthur's men chased the North Korean army up toward the Chinese border, they found themselves facing the huge Chinese army who forced the Americans back. President Harry Truman did not want war with the Chinese and quickly pulled MacArthur back from the war.

Drought and Dust Bowl

A severe lack of rain during the 1930s in the *Great Plains* caused a *drought* that had severe consequences. New motorized farm equipment allowed farmers to plow under grasslands and plant crops on the dry plains where there had been none before. When the drought killed off these crops there was no plant life to hold the soil in place. A huge expanse of land became the great *Dust Bowl*. The winds blew untold amounts of soil over many miles for several years. The huge 100,000,000 acre expanse of land affected by the Dust Bowl went up through Texas and Oklahoma into New Mexico, Colorado, Kansas, and other states. Tens of thousands of families abandoned their farms and faced more hardship trying to find new places to live during the Great Depression.

Eastland Disaster

The Eastland Disaster occurred on July 24, 1915. The Eastland excursion ship was one of the vessels hired to transport people along the southern end of Lake Michigan from Chicago to Michigan City for the Western Electric annual picnic. Western Electric was a large employer that produced telecommunications equipment and services for its parent company AT&T. Making telephones and other related equipment required many thousands of employees at the time.

The company picnic was a day for recreation, fun, and food. However, this day would be one of the saddest days in Chicago history.

While docked on the Chicago River at LaSalle Street, the ship took on 2,500 passengers. The Eastland became unstable and began to "list" or lean. It capsized (turned over on its side) and 844 people were killed.

It was one of the worst naval catastrophes in American history and it occurred just a short distance from shore. More people died in the Eastland disaster than in the Great Chicago Fire of 1871, which was estimated to number about 300.

Farris Wheel

The Eiffel Tower in Paris was built for a world's fair called the 1889 Exposition Universelle. Today it is one of the most popular attractions in France. Daniel Burnham, the Columbian Exhibition's lead architect was seeking something spectacular for the fair in Chicago. George Washington Gale Farris, a structural engineer, who was working on the Columbian Exhibition had the idea of creating a giant wheel with viewing compartments which rotated around a center axle.

Farris was not the first designer of such a wheel, but his design used steel to produce something extraordinary that could carry many people at great heights. His huge Farris Wheel was constructed at the Exhibition. According to the *Smithsonian Magazine*, the original Farris Wheel measured 250 feet in diameter, and carried 36 cars, each capable of holding 60 people. In time, Farris Wheels were created for fairs all over the world. Huge Farris Wheels now can be found as permanent attractions as far away as China.

Franklin Delano Roosevelt

Franklin Delano Roosevelt

The 32nd President of the United States, Franklin Delano Roosevelt (FDR), was elected to his first of four terms in 1932. During his fourth term of office, he died at the closing moments of World War II in 1945.

Roosevelt won election in the early stages of the Great Depression. He implemented policies and programs that were known as the *New Deal* to improve the economy and reduce the suffering of millions of Americans during one of the most difficult periods of our history.

Before becoming president, FDR was stricken with polio. He lost the ability to use his legs and he used braces to walk. He did not want Americans to focus on his disability. Roosevelt did what he could to avoid publicity on it.

He married a distant cousin, Eleanor Roosevelt, who was also related to Theodore Roosevelt. In many ways, Eleanor became one of the most active First Ladies, traveling extensively and reporting back to her husband on the state of the country.

Like Theodore Roosevelt, Franklin Delano Roosevelt was happy to spend much of his life serving his country. Like George Washington and Abraham Lincoln, Roosevelt's presidency took place during tough times when the survival of the United States was at stake.

Galloping Ghost

Red Grange was called the Galloping Ghost. Grantland Rice, one of America's greatest sportswriters, wrote this poetic description of Red Grange:

> A streak of fire, a breath of flame
> Eluding all who reach and clutch;
> A gray ghost thrown into the game
> That rival hands may never touch;
> A rubber bounding, blasting soul
> Whose destination is the goal
> Red Grange of Illinois!

However, it was another sportswriter, Warren Brown, who came up with a nickname for Red Grange: "The Galloping Ghost."

Great Depression

The largest, longest business downturn in history began with the stock market crash in 1929 and lasted in part until the beginning of World War II. At its worst, unemployment was at 25%. People struggled to keep their homes. Many farmers lost their farms. The radio provided shows to help keep people entertained. Inexpensive foods became the norm. It was a time of cutting back on spending for most and a period of great suffering for others.

Buffaloes on Great Plains

Great Plains

The Great Plains is a huge expanse of flatland covered in prairie and grassland west of the Mississippi River and east of the Rocky Mountains. It includes the states of Colorado, Kansas, Montana, Nebraska, New Mexico, North Dakota, Oklahoma, South Dakota, Texas, Wyoming and parts of Canada. In some areas of the Great Plains you can still see the ruts in the ground that show where the covered wagons carried settlers out West on the Oregon Trail.

Harry Truman

Harry Truman

The 33rd President of the United States, Harry Truman, followed Franklin Delano Roosevelt. Unlike Roosevelt who came from wealth, Truman came from the middle class. Truman had fought in World War I and he learned a great deal about leadership in the service. He faced many challenges: Ending the War with Japan; helping to rebuild Europe; responding to communist threats; and facing a new war in Korea.

Truman had witnessed discrimination against black soldiers returning from the war and he introduced measures that produced substantial change in the military and in civil service. Truman also recognized the State of Israel. Truman's presidential style was said to be unpolished, but honest. He had a sign on his desk that stated: "The buck stops here." It was his way of saying, he will make the decisions and you can blame him if you don't like them.

1909 Shredded Wheat Advertisement

"Hitting the curveball"

The curveball is traditionally one of the most challenging pitches to hit in professional baseball because it moves in unexpected ways. It can be a trial for a player moving up from a lower level of play to make the proper adjustments necessary to hit the pitch at a higher level of play.

"Hitting the curveball" is also an "idiom," an expression that means more than the dictionary definition of its words. Someone who is "hitting the curveball" is succeeding at something that is difficult. Someone who can "hit the curveball" separates himself or herself from others.

Foreign-speaking persons have difficulty with idioms. Normally, a foreign-speaking person must learn the meaning of idioms from experience.

Hupmobile

The Hupmobile was built by the Hupp Motor Company in Detroit from 1909 through 1940. In the late 1920s, many Hupmobiles were produced, but the company turned to other ventures in 1940.

The company was started by Robert Hupp. His first car was a little two passenger Runabout. The car company was fairly successful and many Hupmobiles followed. Their offerings grew from two passenger vehicles, to three, and four.

A four passenger touring model traveled around the world in 1910-1912. In 1916, another Hupmobile made a trip through all 48 states. The company continued through much of the Depression. A labor dispute led to no new models being manufactured in 1937. A promising new Skylark debuted in 1939, but the company ended its car manufacturing in 1940.

The company continued to manufacture parts for the war effort in the 1940s and made parts for other companies as well. It morphed into a manufacturer of parts for appliances, heating, and cooling equipment and other industrial parts until it disappeared in the 1990s.

Hyperbole

Hyperbole is extravagant exaggeration—not just exaggerating a little bit but exaggerating so much so that people immediately know you are stretching the truth. This is done in sports reporting to entertain. In football, former NFL quarterback Peyton Manning could throw the ball "a mile;" the defensive line of the Minnesota Vikings were "purple people eaters;" and the Chicago Bears are the "monsters of the midway."

Jordan

The Jordan Motor Car Company produced cars from 1916 to 1931. The company, operated out of Cleveland. It was especially remarkable for its marketing and advertising. It offered several colors and models like the "Sport Machine" and the "Tomboy."

League

A league is an association or relationship of people or groups that are organized together for a common purpose. The primary reason for a league of professional football teams was to help members schedule games that could be promoted in advance. A league can also provide structure and rules to enforce actions that benefit all those involved.

Misgivings

Misgivings are feelings of suspicion or a lack of trust. If you have misgivings about a project, a program, or some work you are involved in, you may not do as well as if you have confidence in these things. If a teammate has misgivings about the teams' goals or objectives, he may not play well.

Missed the boat

"Missed the boat" is an *idiom*: an expression that means more than the dictionary definition of its words. Missed the boat can mean that someone was "too late to make a boat trip," but as an idiom, it can also mean that someone failed to take advantage of an opportunity. Halas really did miss the boat and was too late to catch the Eastland before it sank! But some athletes "miss the boat" by not working hard enough at training and exercise. Others like Walter Payton achieve a level of fitness through exercise that is greatly admired.

Modified T Formation

A football formation is a type of arrangement used at the start of a play. The T Formation uses a quarterback directly behind the center, a fullback behind the quarterback, and two halfbacks on either side of the fullback all forming a "T" behind the line of scrimmage.

The T Formation is one of the oldest formations in football. With four men in the backfield, the formation allowed for a number of variations on handoffs, fakes, pass patterns from the backfield, etc. The essential weakness in the T Formation was that defenses could focus on the center of the field.

The Modified T Formation made use of a man in motion and other elements that spread the action across the field and made it much more difficult to defend. The Modified T Formation was created decades after the original T Formation.

New Deal

The New Deal was a collection of programs that Franklin Delano Roosevelt introduced to help Americans during the Great Depression and beyond. These include the Works Progress Administration (WPA) that employed millions of Americans, the Social Security Administration that helped Americans in retirement, and many laws that helped reform the banking system and aid people in their jobs and on the farm.

NFL Schedules

In the first decade of the NFL, the League was establishing itself and working out some consistency with the member teams and their schedules. At first, the number of games played varied from team-to-team. Teams formed and disbanded quickly. Of the inaugural season teams, only the Decatur Staleys/Chicago Bears and the Chicago/Saint Louis/Arizona Cardinals survived. Stronger Markets were added and eventually the schedules were made consistent.

On September 24, 1933, the Bears opened the season with a 14—7 win over the Green Bay Packers. In 1933, the NFL went to a consistent 11-game schedule that would last until the war years.

On September 26, 1943, the Bears and Packers opened the 10-game season in a 21—21 tie. The War was taking its toll on the NFL and there were only eight active teams that year.

On September 29, 1946, the Bears opened the 11-game season with a 30–7 win over the Green Bay Packers. Sid Luckman was the Bears quarterback.
On September 28, 1947, the Bears would open the 12-game season losing to the Green Bay Packers, 29–20. The NFL would stick to a 12-game schedule until 1961.

On September 17, 1961, the Chicago Bears began their season by playing the Minnesota Vikings. The NFL regular schedule began a week earlier than the previous season as teams adjusted to their new 14-game regular season. It was the expansion-team Vikings first game of their inaugural season. They beat the Bears, 37-13, with Fran Tarkenton's 17 completions on 23 attempts for 250 yards and 4 touchdowns. Beating the Bears in the opener was a good first step for the franchise, but the Vikings would end up 3–13 for the season including a 52-35 loss to the Bears on the December 17.

On September 3, 1978, the Chicago Bears began their first 16-game season by playing the Saint Louis Cardinals. The NFL regular schedule began 2 weeks earlier than the previous season as teams adjusted to the longer regular season. The Bears beat the Cardinals, 17-10. Bob Avellini was the Bears starting quarterback and Walter Payton and Roland Harper combined for 194 yards.

Optimum

Optimum is something that is the best or most favorable. An optimum effort is one that cannot be improved.

Pacific

The Pacific theater or Pacific operation in World War II included war efforts in the Pacific Ocean. Battles centered on the Philippines as well as various islands between Japan and Hawaii. Battles for control of the islands were particularly brutal. Naval battles involved significant resources and men.

Pearl Harbor

Pearl Harbor is an American Naval Base near Honolulu, Hawaii. On December 7, 1941, hundreds of Japanese fighter planes attacked the base to destroy many ships including eight massive battleships. About 200 airplanes were destroyed. More than 2,000 American soldiers and sailors were killed with more than 1,000 wounded. Roosevelt would describe the attack as a "day of infamy." The day after the assault, President Franklin D. Roosevelt asked Congress to declare war on Japan.

Perilous

Something that is perilous involves risk or danger. In the early days of football, the game was thought to be perilous. In the early 20th century, deaths and serious injuries ran high among participating players. President Theodore Roosevelt encouraged reforms and changes were made that outlawed dangerous mass formations, encouraged the pass, and made other improvements that made the game safer.

Postwar Difficulties for the NFL

After World War II had come to an end, difficult times remained for the NFL. Arch Ward, a powerful Chicago Tribune Sports Editor, formed a new league, the All-American Football Conference (AAFC) that operated during the 1946-1949 NFL seasons. Former NFL players were sought after by the new league. The AAFC also competed with the NFL for players coming out of college. Financially, NFL teams were hurt by competition with AAFC teams in cities that had teams from both leagues.

AAFC teams had their problems as well. The Cleveland Browns dominated its competition in the new league and several of the lesser teams had difficulty holding on to fan support. Late in 1949, NFL Commissioner Bert Bell announced a merger agreement. Under the agreement, the AAFC Cleveland Browns, San Francisco 49ers, and Baltimore Colts would join the NFL in 1950. Other AAFC teams would disband. A new organization was established to group the Browns, Cardinals, Eagles, Giants, Redskins, and Steelers in the American Conference and the Bears, Colts, 49ers, Lions, Packers, Rams, and Yanks in the National Conference.

Prototype

A prototype is the accepted norm or a typical example of something. It can also be a model or sample for a new product or offering.

Rose Bowl

The Rose Bowl Game is an annual American college football bowl game played at the start of the New Year in the Rose Bowl stadium in Pasadena, California. The Pasadena Tournament of Roses annual parade takes place before the Rose Bowl Game and is watched live by hundreds of thousands of people. Millions more watch it on television.

The Rose Bowl game is the oldest currently operating bowl game. It began in 1902. Conference champions from the Big Ten and Pac-12 conferences (or their predecessors) are usually invited. During World War I and World War II, teams from military bases played in the Rose Bowl. Today, the college football national championship system can impact the Rose Bowl in some years.

Running boards

Running boards are narrow steps or foot boards usually attached to the side of a car or truck that people can step on when getting in or out. They were common on many old cars, but they are often seen on pickup trucks today.

Starch

Starch is a white powdery substance found in plants. It is plentiful in cereal plants such as corn and wheat. Many things we eat include starch. Starch serves as a kind of emergency energy storage for plants. It also works this way in people by releasing some of the sugar absorbed with starch when it is needed. Starch is also a thickener and it is used for many products such as spray starch for removing wrinkles from shirts, laundry products and more. The Staley Manufacturing Company obtained its starch largely from corn.

Symbolism/Symbolic/Symbolically

Sometimes a word or action can be a symbol of something. It suggests something other than what it normally means. When words or actions are used in this way they are symbolic of something else and we call this symbolism. Symbolism is used in literature, paintings, plays, and movies. If you see a dove in a painting, the artist might be trying to convey a sense of peace. "Dark clouds" in a book might suggest that there is trouble on the way. Water is often a symbol of life.

A trip or pilgrimage can also be a metaphor for life's journey. Sometimes a trip teaches us something important about our lives that might have been otherwise difficult to see in our everyday living.

Theodore Roosevelt

Theodore "Teddy" Roosevelt

President Theodore Roosevelt was the 26th President of the United States. He became President after William McKinley was assassinated in 1901. Roosevelt was elected for a second term on November 8, 1904. He held the office from March 1901 to March 1909.

Roosevelt was one of our most energetic Presidents. He was an author, a naturalist, soldier, explorer, and a historian. He was also a distant cousin of President Franklin Roosevelt and an uncle to Eleanor Roosevelt. Roosevelt won the Nobel Peace Prize and the Medal of Honor. His image is depicted on Mount Rushmore along with George Washington, Thomas Jefferson, and Abraham Lincoln.

Several National Parks and National Monuments were created when Roosevelt was President. He wrote dozens of books. As a young boy he was sickly, but he took on strenuous exercise to become fit.

Trench Warfare

Trench warfare is land warfare that involves troops digging in and mostly residing in trenches to shield themselves from artillery. It's warfare of limited movement. Large numbers of soldiers were killed in such conditions during World War I. During the war poisonous gas was used by both sides in trench warfare. And in some cases men dug tunnels a hundred feet under their enemy's trenches and set off huge underground mines. Today in parts of Europe, some trenches dug in World War I, can be seen with the huge holes created by mines.

Hutchinson Hall, University of Chicago

University of Chicago

The University of Chicago is a private university in Chicago that is ranked with the best schools in the country. It sits on 215 acres in the Hyde Park area of Chicago. It was built on land donated by Marshall Field, the department store founder, with funds in part donated by John D. Rockefeller, who co-founded the Standard Oil Company. About 16,500 students attend. University of Chicago faculty, scholars, students, and alumni are renowned for the highest international honors in their fields.

The University of Chicago has several landmark buildings. Hutchison Hall is one of those. Hutchinson Hall's dining hall was modeled after a medieval one at the University of Oxford that was replicated in a London studio for the Harry Potter movie series.

President Obama's home in Chicago is less than a mile for the University of Chicago's modern ship-like Gerald Ratner Athletics Center. The site of the Obama Presidential Library is steps away from the University of Chicago.

WPA Art Poster

University of Illinois, Urbana-Champaign

The University of Illinois is located in the twin cities of Champaign and Urbana 140 miles south of Chicago. It is one of the original 37 public land-grant institutions created after President Abraham Lincoln signed the Morrill Act in 1862. The University of Illinois is the flagship institution of the University of Illinois system. It is known throughout the world for its quality education and attracts many foreign students among the 50,000 students that attend the University.

The number of University of Illinois football players who have competed in the NFL is approaching 300. Famous Bears' players who attended Illinois include George Halas, Red Grange, Dick Butkus, and Ed O'Bradovich. Former Bears Head Coach Lovie Smith is the current Head Coach of the Illini.

Vintage

Vintage is a period of origin, a time of original manufacture of an item that is fine. A time when something was at its best and long lasting. Examples: *The vintage 1964 Mustang commands a high price. A vintage blanket chest made in Massachusetts in the 17th century is likely to be found in a museum today.*

Photographer Walker Evans

Walker Evans

Walker Evans was an American photographer who used photographs to tell stories (a photojournalist). His photographs taken during the Great Depression when working for the Farm Security Administration are among his most admired. Evans photographs of poor tenant families in southern Alabama were published in a book called *Let Us Now Praise Famous Men* that was written by James Agee a Pulitzer Prize winning author.

Western Electric

Western Electric was a large company that made telephone parts and supplies for American Telephone and Telegraph Company (ATT). The Western Electric Hawthorne plant in Cicero, Illinois, where George Halas had a job, employed as many as 45,000 people.

Who Do We Play Next Week?

If you watch the great coaches during a game, you can see the intensity at times. Sometimes it is a quiet kind of burn, but coaches are certainly "in the moment." George Halas would roam up and down the sidelines and manage his team like it was part of him. His strong hands would latch onto the back of a player's jersey and he would thrust the player into the game. It was all real, all now, and all personal. But when a game ended, it was finished. His quote, "Who do we play next week," was Halas's way of inspiring those around him to look forward, not backward.

Win, Lose, or Draw

In a game, you can win, lose, or draw (tie). "Win, Lose, or Draw" also refers to a very popular newspaper column by Warren Brown. Brown wrote about sports for many years in his column and then named his 1947 book *Win, Lose, or Draw* after his column. Brown also wrote other books: *Rockne*, *The Chicago Cubs*, and *The Chicago White Sox*.

World War I

World War I was a global military conflict that took place from 1914-1918. Nations that formed the Allied powers (Great Britain, France, Russia, Italy, United States, and others) fought the Central powers (Germany, Austria-Hungary, Turkey, Bulgaria). Nationalism, the belief that people of the same ethnic type, language, and political ideas should be allowed to form their own governments, was one cause of conflicts. Imperialism, the policy and effort to expand by diplomacy or force one country's power and control into foreign markets was another cause of hostilities. As tensions increased in part from growing nationalism and imperialism, countries expanded their military operations. A local war between Austria-Hungary and Serbia began with the assassination of Austria Archduke Francis Ferdinand by a Serb nationalist. Fallout from that event expanded onto the major conflict we call World War I.

President Kennedy Throws out Ball at All-Star Game

World War II

Ending World War I was the Treaty of Versailles that contributed to almost impossible post war conditions in Germany that helped fuel power struggles between the government and other political groups. Three groups supporting radical dictatorship and nationalism came to power in Germany, Italy, and Japan. These countries formed the Axis powers and began to expand their boundaries by force. Germany invaded Poland. Great Britain and France, two Allied countries, were drawn into the war.

When the Japanese attacked Pearl Harbor, the United States was drawn in on the side of the Allies. President Dwight Eisenhower, President Richard Nixon, President Gerald Ford, President John Kennedy, President George H. W. Bush, and President Jimmy

Carter (Midshipman U. S. Naval Academy) all served in the military during the war. The Japanese surrendered on September 2, 1945, aboard the USS Missouri to end the war.

World's Columbian Exposition

The 1893 Chicago World's Fair or the World's Columbian Exposition was held in Jackson Park and on the Midway Plaisance in Chicago to celebrate the 400th anniversary of the arrival of Christopher Columbus in the New World in 1492. The exhibition opened in 1893, a year later than anticipated. People were impressed by the sights and scenes of the event. Some 27.5 million came to see it. It cost more than $31 million to put it on. There were some 65,000 exhibitions. Jackson Park was where the exhibition area was located. Midway Plaisance was where most entertainment facilities were placed. Nearly 700 acres of beautiful parks and grounds provided exhibitions, music, food, and more. States at the time had their own buildings to exhibit displays, Many countries were represented with their own buildings as well.

MILWAUKEE							5				2				2
CINCINNATI							7							
PHILADELPHIA							4				OUT	
WASHINGTON							2				2	
PITTSBURGH	0	I	I	0	0	I	I					
CUBS	4	0	2	0	0	0				VIS	7	HITS	7	CUB
INNING	1	2	3	4	5	6	7	8	9	10

Wrigley Field Hand-Operated Scoreboard

Wrigley Field

Wrigley Field is the famous baseball park known for its ivy-covered brick outfield wall, it's hand operated scoreboard, and its beautiful natural setting on the north side of Chicago a few miles from downtown. The Chicago Bears Football Club called Wrigley Field home from 1921 to 1970. The Field was originally built for Charles Weeghman's Chicago Whales professional baseball team of the Federal League. It was referred to as Weeghman Park. After the league folded, the Chicago Cubs started playing there and within a few years, William Wrigley, Jr., a man who made a fortune selling chewing gum, owned the team. For a while it was referred to as Cubs Park. Eventually, the field was named Wrigley Field after its owner.

Patrick McCaskey

Decorative Image from Library of Congress
Reading Room

Quiz

Here's a quiz on *Papa Bear and the Chicago Bears' Winning Ways*.

1. The A. E. Staley Manufacturing Company was what kind of company?
a) Farm equipment
b) Agribusiness
c) Cereal
d) Entertainment

2. George Halas played for what Major League Baseball Team?
a) Chicago Cubs
b) Chicago White Sox
c) New York Yankees
d) Detroit Tigers

3. The Eastland Disaster was the result of what type of accident?
a) Capsizing
b) Run aground
c) Hitting an iceberg
d) Fire caused by lightning

4. World War I involved what horrific type of combat?
a) Long range bombers
b) Nuclear submarines
c) Trench warfare

5. World War I occurred in what century?
a) Nineteenth
b) Eighteenth
c) Twentieth
d. Seventeenth

6. When World War I started, Halas joined which branch of military service?
a) Army
b) Navy
c) Air Force
d) Marines

7. Pro football's organizational meeting in Canton was held at Ralph Hay's automobile showroom. When there weren't enough chairs to go around, some attendees found a seat on bumpers and running boards of what make of car that Hay sold?
a) Chevrolet
b) Hupmobile
c) Oldsmobile
d) Rambler

8. When the Staley's moved from Decatur to Chicago what stadium did they play in originally?
a) Comisky Park
b) Dexter Park
c) Cubs Park (Wrigley Field)
d) Soldier Field

9. Who were the first "Monsters of the Midway?"
a) University of Illinois
b) Chicago Bears
c) Chicago Cardinals
d) University of Chicago

10. What tragic event occurred on the Great Plains during the Great Depression?
a) Johnstown Flood
b) Dust Bowl
c) Chicago Fire
d) San Francisco earthquake

11. Who gave Fireside Chats on the radio during the Great Depression?
a) Teddy Roosevelt
b) Ronald Reagan
c) Harry Truman
d) Franklin Delano Roosevelt

12. The tragic Bombing of Pearl Harbor began our involvement in World War II. Within a week we were at war against 3 countries. We were not at war with which country below?
a) China
b) Japan
c) Italy
d) Germany

13. What did Walker Evans do for a living?
a) Senator
b) Fought forest fires
c) Photographer
d) Football coach

14. What did Western Electric make?
a) Footballs
b) Telephone equipment
c) Automobiles
d) Uniforms

15. What releases sugar in plants when it is needed?

a) Earth worms

b) Chocolate

c) Starch

d) Salt

16. The Rose Bowl is normally played in what city?

a) New York, NY

b) Pasadena, CA

c) Holland, MI

d) Des Moines, IA

17. The Columbian Exhibition celebrated what?

a) The naming of the Columbia River in the Pacific Northwest.

b) Colombia becoming an independent country in South America.

c) The founding of the Columbia Phonograph company.

d) Christopher Columbus coming to America.

18. Which one of these **is not** an appropriate use of the word "misgivings?"

a) Henry had misgivings about joining the choir.

b) When his rival nominated him for class president, Benny had misgivings about the election at school.

c) Sometimes you give someone something they appreciate. Other times you make misgivings.

d) Shy students had misgivings over exchanging Valentines in class so their teacher stopped the practice.

19. What do we call the huge expanse of flat land covered in prairie and grassland west of the Mississippi River and east of the Rocky Mountains?

a) Summer solstice

b) Tornado alley

c) Great Plains

d) Bread bowl

20. In life "hitting the curveball" is doing something difficult. What are the difficult things that George Halas did in his life?

a) He served our country in times of war.

b) He kept his team going during the Great Depression.

c) In good times and bad times, he always looked forward to the future and never got too discouraged.

d) All of the above.

21. Which President below served in the military in World War I **not** in World War II?

a) Gerald Ford

b) Richard Nixon

c. John Kennedy

d) Harry Truman

22. Which Chicago chewing gum company executive owned the Chicago Cubs?

a) Charles Weeghman

b) Marshall Field

c) William Wrigley

d) Daniel Burnham

23. What are some of the features fans enjoy at Wrigley Field?

a) Ivy covered outfield walls.

b) Hand operated scoreboard.

c) Location in the city of Chicago.

d) All of the above.

24. Hutchinson Hall at the University of Chicago was modeled after Christ Church, one of the Colleges of Oxford University in England. The dining hall at Christ Church was replicated in a London movie studio for what films?

a) Harry Potter

b) Batman

c) A Hard Day's Night

d) James Bond

25. The line, "We'll never forget the way you thrilled the nation with your T formation," is from what song?

a) Notre Dame Fight Song

b) On Wisconsin

c) Go! You Packers, Go!

d) Bear down, Chicago Bears

Exercise on Franklin's Virtues

Earlier in this book, we talked about Franklin's list of virtues and how he established habits using his charts. Like many of our founding fathers, Franklin was disciplined and self-reliant. For Franklin, his list of important virtues included temperance, silence, order, resolution, frugality, industry, sincerity, justice, moderation, cleanliness, tranquility, chastity, and humility. Some of Franklin's language may not be clear to you. Here is a brief explanation of his virtues taken from his autobiography:

1. Temperance: Eat and drink sensibly.
2. Silence: Speak when speech is helpful.
3. Order: Have a proper place and time for everything.
4. Resolution: Perform what you ought.
5. Frugality. Spend only to do good to others or yourself.
6. Industry: Be employed in something useful.
7. Sincerity: Think and speak kindly/innocently.
8. Justice: Wrong no one and do your duty.
9. Moderation: Avoid extremes.
10. Cleanliness: Keep your body, clothes, and home clean.
11. Tranquility: Don't let small things disturb you.
12. Chastity: Be pure of heart and respect others.
13. Humility: Imitate unpretentious people (Franklin's examples were Jesus and Socrates).

Talk to your parents about virtues that they were brought up with in their lives. Show them Franklin's list and work with them to create a list that would be important for you. After your discussion with your parents, write down your thoughts on living a virtuous life.

Franklin's virtues suggest someone who advocated living a disciplined life. He wrote "speak kindly," but he also wrote "do your duty." He was often involved in difficult negotiations. The period of time just before the Revolutionary War was difficult, the War was difficult, and after the War there were many problems that needed solving for the United States to survive. Just before signing the Declaration of Independence, Franklin said: "We must, indeed, all hang together, or most assuredly we shall all hang separately."

Edward Kemeys's Guardian Lions,

Chicago Art Institute

Discussion Questions

Discussion questions help you process information that you are learning. Here are some questions that will help you do that. These might be used in class, you might want to think about them on your own, or you might want to talk to your parents to get their ideas as well.

1. Big events in history can sometimes teach us important things. As a society, what can we learn from the dustbowl about conservation? What can we learn from the Great Depression about taking risks with money and savings?

2. It has been said that people who pay no attention to history, repeat it. Are there current events that you study in class that remind you of events in history?

3. Franklin Delano Roosevelt and Theodore Roosevelt came from wealthy families who taught them at a young age that focusing their energies on the common good was something to which to aspire. Both men had great setbacks in their lives, but they demonstrated courage to achieve goals. We may not know presidents or war heroes, but are there people you know who have overcome adversity to help others?

4. People can take things that look old and create something new and inspiring. Halas and his coaches did this by modifying the T Formation. Can you think of a song, play, or movie that looks at a past event and makes it seem new?

5. Sometimes there are unintended consequences from changes meant to improve things. When the Eastland capsized some believed this was the result of a law that required more lifeboats, which may have made the ship top-heavy. Unintended consequences is one reason why parents take time to think things over. Can you remember a time when you disagreed with your parents about something that you felt strongly about, but you found out later, they were right?

6. Halas had the idea that we should be disciplined about what we practice—to practice only those things we use in the game. It says something about how we should prepare for most everything. If we spend most of our time wasting time, do you think we will be ready for life's challenges?

7. Competitors take away their oppositions' strengths in sports. Kids who are cruel to others can sometimes be encouraged by the laughs they get. What do you think would happen if people stopped laughing when others are cruel?

8. Halas suggested that people who give their best don't regret it. Many people talk about how they didn't apply themselves in school. They goofed around too much and didn't study the way they should have. They regret it. But you don't hear many adults saying they worked too hard in school. What does that say to you?

9. Actor Bob Denver played a funny character called Maynard G. Krebs on the "Dobbie Gillis" TV Series. When Maynard said the word "work," he said it with a squeal because he hated work so much. Life would have been so much simpler for Maynard if he adjusted his attitude. Work is the effort we put into tasks. When we decide we'd rather be doing something else, the effort can become for us like Maynard's idea of "work." As you get older you will prepare for a career and if you choose the right one for you, it will likely go well as long as you don't find yourself thinking that you'd rather be doing something else. What are the things you work very hard at that you enjoy, but some of your friends call "work?"

10. Halas's advice about never going to bed a loser is critical. If we are moving towards goals for ourselves, we should try to make progress every day. Each night we should look back at our day and adjust our plans for tomorrow. Talk to someone you know who has done well and ask them about Halas's advice.

Bonus Questions

11. Photojournalism is the work photographers do to produce images used in news stories and other media. Just like a print reporter, photojournalists face certain moral considerations in their work. Can you and your classmates think of any?

12. Virtues are often written about together. A virtuous person does not just practice a few virtues! Franklin's system was created to encourage his habits of practicing many virtues. You often see lists of good habits together. Many

of us may find it easy to practice some good behaviors and find it much harder to practice others. Talk to your classmates and find out what habits they think are most difficult to practice. Is there any consensus about which are easiest and which are hardest?

13. Successful Pro Athletes can find it difficult to practice good habits that relate to their spending money (frugality) and their diets (temperance). A 300-pound lineman may need to lose a third of his body weight after his career is over! But players who set out goals in advance are more likely to achieve results. Planning to achieve goals might help you manage the success that you may have in the future. Write down some goals that you would like to achieve when you start your own career. Talk to your friends and classmates to see what they might have in mind for their goals.

14. You hear much about athletes who overcome adversity or challenges. Often they need to make adjustments in their play. Sometime they need to make a quick recovery from an injury. In this book you read about Theodore and Franklin Roosevelt. Theodore was a sickly child and had to work extra hard to get in good physical shape. Franklin's legs were paralyzed. It must have been very difficult for him each and every day. But many Americans were not aware of his trials. Talk to your friends and classmates about people that you admire for overcoming hardships.

15. Think of stories about relatives of yours who have overcome great hardships? Sometimes these are discovered when a family member does research on your family tree. Share those with your classmates and friends. Take the time to listen carefully to classmates' and friends' stories. Are there similarities between yours and theirs even though you may come from different backgrounds?

Virtue, Liberty, and Independence Relief

Photo and Illustrations Credits

All photographs are reproduced with permission (unless public domain).

Page	Description	Source
Cover	George Halas	Bill Potter
Page iv	George Halas Montage	Bill Potter
Page vi	Author, Patrick McCaskey	Jonathan Daniel
Page 3	World War I Poster, James Montgomery	Library of Congress
Page 5	Hupmobile	Library of Congress
Page 8	Midway Columbian Exhibition	Library of Congress
Page 11	Young Worker, photo by Walker Evans	Library of Congress
Page 12	Dust Bowl Farm, photo by Arthur Rothstein	Library of Congress
Page 14	FDR Fireside Chat, Harris & Ewing Photographs	Library of Congress,
Page 15	Federal Emergency Relief Administration, camps in Atlanta	National Archives and Records Administration (NARA)
Page 16	USS Indianapolis	United States Navy
Page 18	World War II Poster, Lawrence Beall Smith	Library of Congress
Page 23	Red Grange	Library of Congress
Page 36	George Halas	Bill Potter

Patrick McCaskey

Page	Description	Source
Page 48	President Obama throws football in Soldier Field, photo by Pete Souza	White House
Page 49	Benjamin Franklin, Maurin Lithograph of painting by Joseph-Siffrède Duplessis	Library of Congress
Page 68	Franklin Delano Roosevelt painting by Francis Owen Salisbury	Official Presidential Portrait
Page 71	Buffaloes on Great Plains, photo by Jeff Zylland	National Park Service
Page 72	Harry Truman painting by Greta Kempton	Official Presidential Portrait
Page 73	Shredded Wheat Advertisement	Library of Congress
Page 84	Theodore Roosevelt painting by John Singer Sargent	Official Presidential Portrait
Page 86	Hutchison Hall, University of Chicago, Detroit Publishing Company	Library of Congress
Page 88	WPA Art Poster	Library of Congress
Page 90	Walker Evans, photo by Edwin Locke, for the Farm Security Administration,	Library of Congress
Page 93	President Kennedy tossing first ball at 1962 Major League All-Star Baseball Game, photo by Cecil William Stoughton	U.S. National Archives and Records Administration

WINNING WAYS

Page	Description	Source
Page 95	Wrigley Field Hand-Operated Scoreboard	D. Benjamin Miller
Page 96	Decorative Image, Library of Congress Reading Room, photo by Carol Highsmith	Library of Congress
Page 106	Edward Kemeys's Guardian Lions, Chicago Art Institute, photo by Carol Highsmith	Library of Congress
Page 112	Decorative historical tablet on Forum Building home of the State Library of Pennsylvania, photo by Carol Highsmith	Library of Congress
Page 116	World War II Soldiers awaiting train at Union Station in Chicago, photo by Jack Delano, Farm Security Administration	Library of Congress
Page 123	Reflecting Pool on the National Mall, photo of Carol Highsmith	Library of Congress
Various	Chicago Bears Helmet	Daniel Norris

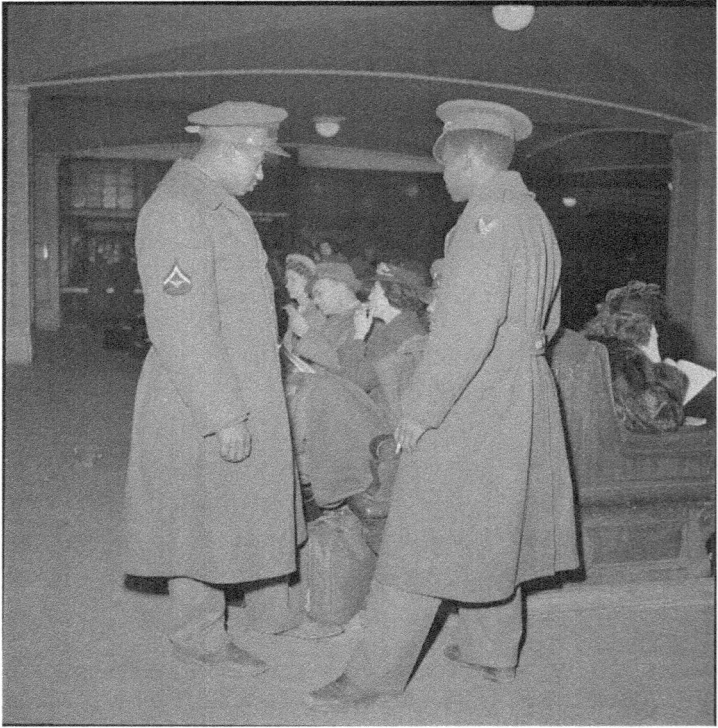

World War II Soldiers Awaiting Train

Index

Reflecting Pool on the National Mall

Patrick McCaskey

Patrick McCaskey was born at Saint Francis Hospital in Evanston. He played basketball and baseball for Saint Mary's School in Des Plaines. He played football and ran track for Notre Dame High School in Niles. He ran cross-country and track for Cheshire Academy in Connecticut. Pat's mom and dad had 11 children: 3 girls and 8 boys. His parents encouraged faith, hard work, reading, and a good laugh.

Pat was a contributing editor to the literary magazines at Loyola University in Chicago and Indiana University. He started working for the Chicago Bears in 1974. He went to DePaul University at night during the off-seasons and earned a master's degree.

Pat is a Chicago Bears' Board Member and a Bears' Vice President. He is the Chairman of Sports Faith International which recognizes people who are successful in sports while leading exemplary lives. Sports Faith has a radio station, WSFI, 88.5 FM, which broadcasts in northern Illinois and southern Wisconsin.

Pat is the author of many books including:
Bear with Me: A Family History of George Halas and the Chicago Bears;
Sports and Faith: Stories of the Devoted and the Devout;
Pillars of the NFL: Coaches Who Have Won Three or More Championships;
Sports and Faith: More Stories of the Devoted and the Devout;
Pilgrimage;
Worthwhile Struggle;
Sportsmanship; and
Papa Bear and the Chicago Bears' Winning Ways.

Pat and his wife, Gretchen, have three sons: Ed, Tom, and Jim; two daughters in law: Elizabeth and Emily; three granddaughters: Grace, Charlotte, and Violet Min; and a grandson, Pat.